On the news it said there would be lots of shooting stars that night. Nadim had come to watch in the back garden with Biff and Chip.

"Shooting stars aren't real stars," Mum explained. "They're bits of rock from space that burn up as they come close to Earth."

The children gazed up at the night sky.

"What if we saw alien spaceships instead of shooting stars?" said Chip.

"Let's hope they'd be nice, friendly aliens!" laughed Biff.

Nadim grinned. He loved films and books about spaceships and aliens.

"In most science fiction stories, aliens don't just come to say hello," Nadim said. "Sometimes they come to invade Earth!"

Biff shivered. "I hope those aliens don't mind cold weather then," she said. "It's getting chilly. Let's go in and get our jackets."

When they went upstairs, Nadim noticed a glow
from behind Biff's door.

"It's the magic key," he said. "I wonder where
it's going to take us this time."

"We'll soon find out!" said Biff, as the magic
whisked them away.

They found themselves outside under a different star-filled sky.

Chip pointed to several buildings nearby. "Look," he said. "We're on a farm."

Biff and Nadim were not looking where Chip was pointing.

"Look!" cried Nadim. "There's a shooting star!"

The children watched the shooting star as it streaked across the sky.

"That's odd," said Nadim. "It isn't burning up."

Suddenly they heard a voice behind them.
The children turned to see a big teenager shining a torch at them.

"Who are you? What are you doing on my Pa's land?" he said.

Before the children could answer him, there was a strange noise from above them.

Everybody looked up. The light in the dark sky looked like a ball of fire now.

"It's going to hit the ground!" shouted Biff.

There was a booming sound as the fireball landed on the far side of the barn.

"Let's go and see," said Nadim.

"Wait!" The teenager held up one hand. "This is Wilkins Farm, and *I'm* Hank Wilkins. I'm going first."

Hank set off and the children followed him.

When they reached the field, they gasped.
A perfectly round object sat in the middle of a
hole in the ground. Smoke was rising from it.

"That isn't a bit of rock," said Biff. "Look.
It's smooth and silver."

"This is just like a science fiction film!"
said Nadim.

Suddenly there was a hissing sound and a door appeared in the side of the silver ball.

The children watched in amazement as a strange little creature flopped out on to the ground.

Hank stepped forward and said, "What are *you* doing on my Pa's land?"

The strange creature looked at them with huge eyes and clasped its bony hands together.

"Please, help me!" it said. "My name is Mendax and I'm in terrible, terrible danger. You must hide me before they come and find me!"

"Before *who* come and find you?" demanded Hank.

Mendax pointed a long, trembling finger up
to the skies.

The children looked up and saw a much bigger
light approaching.

"Please help!" repeated Mendax. "The
Grozzers are chasing me. Hide me! *Please!*"

After a few seconds' thought, Hank nodded
slowly. "Pa's truck is over near the barn," he said.
"We can hide behind that."

As they ran, a strange humming sound came
from the sky. It got louder and louder.

"Their spaceship's going to land!" wailed Mendax.

As the children hid, a huge, disc-shaped object hovered in the sky. It landed next to the crater that Mendax's ship had made.

"The Grozzers have been after me for days," Mendax whispered. "They're very dangerous!"

A door in the Grozzers' ship opened and several new aliens marched out. These were much bigger and scarier than Mendax.

One of them started looking at Mendax's little spaceship.

"I don't like the look of this," said Nadim quietly.

Mendax trembled. "Is there a town nearby?"
he asked. "The Grozzers won't be able to find me
in a busy place like that."

"The town's just down the road," said Hank,
pointing. "But I'm not sure you'll get there before
they catch you."

Mendax smiled broadly, showing his sharp little teeth. "I might be able to get away if you can distract them," he said.

"Won't that be dangerous?" asked Hank.

Mendax shook his head. "The Grozzers don't care about you. They only want to catch me."

Biff nodded bravely. "You three do your best to distract the Grozzers," she said. "I'll take Mendax as far as the main road into town. I'll be back in ten minutes."

She ran off with Mendax towards the road.

Chip and Nadim glanced towards the Grozzers' ship. The aliens were starting to search the area.

"We need a brilliant idea to distract them," said Chip.

Hank ran forwards, waving his arms around and shouting, "Hey! Over here!" at the top of his voice.

There was nothing Chip and Nadim could do except follow Hank and join in.

"This way, Grozzers!" shouted Nadim.

"Come and get us!" shouted Chip.

Moments later a few of the Grozzers zipped up to them on scooters that hovered just above the ground.

The first Grozzer lifted its goggles and fixed the boys with blazing red eyes. "Where can we find Mendax?" it demanded. "Tell us."

"He's gone," said Nadim firmly. "You've missed him and now you'll never catch him."

The Grozzers looked suddenly worried.
"That's terrible," the second one said. "Once
Mendax has learned all about your world, he will
send a report to his home planet. Then his people
will invade your little world."

Nadim was shocked. "You mean, *Mendax*
wants to take over planet Earth?"

"Quick!" said Chip. "Mendax is on his way to the town, and my sister Biff is with him!"

"We must stop him!" said the Grozzers. "Mendax can change his appearance to look like any other living creature. If he reaches town, we'll lose him forever. Let's go!"

Biff was close to the main road now, but she
slowed down when she heard a strange noise
behind her.

She turned round and gasped. Mendax was not
there. Instead, an exact copy of Biff herself was
staring back at her.

"What's going on?" asked Biff.

"Silence, Earth child!" commanded the Biff
look-alike with a nasty grin.

"Is that you, Mendax?" asked Biff.

"Of course!" answered the copy of Biff. "Even
if the Grozzers catch us, they'll arrest *you*, not *me*!
Nothing will stop my people from taking over Earth!"

Moments later the Grozzers zoomed up on their hover-scooters. The two Biffs turned to meet them.

"Which one is Mendax?" demanded one Grozzer.

"That's Mendax!" said one Biff, pointing angrily.

"No!" said the other Biff, also pointing. "*That's* Mendax!"

The first Grozzer turned to his companion.
He whispered, "We must ask something that only
an Earth person would get right."

The second Grozzer nodded, then said, "How
did you arrive at this place?"

"I came on my bike," said one Biff quickly.

"That's not true," said the other Biff. "Mendax landed in a spaceship. And I . . . well, a magic key brought me here."

The Grozzers looked at each other. "Our files say bikes are a common form of transport here," said one. "We have no record of 'magic keys'."

A Grozzer turned to the real Biff. "Come with us, Mendax," it said. "We're taking you home."

"Wait!" shouted a voice behind them. "There really is a magic key!"

Chip was running down the lane as fast as he could. Nadim and Hank were not far behind.

Once the boys arrived, Mendax knew that his chance to escape was over. With a shimmer of light, he returned to his normal form.

Mendax screwed up his nose as he looked around. "I'm not sure I even want to invade this place any more," he sniffed.

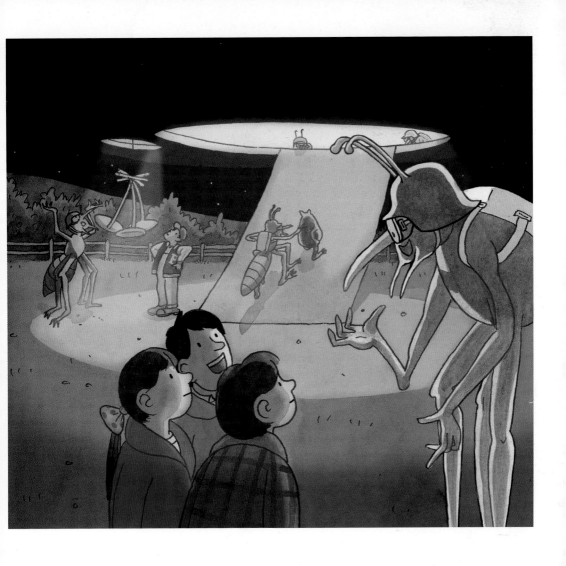

They went back to the Grozzer ship.

"Mendax is safely on board," explained one Grozzer. "Thanks for your help, Earth children."

"Will you visit our planet again?" asked Nadim.

"Perhaps," said the second Grozzer. "When you humans are ready for it . . ."

The children watched as the Grozzers' ship took off, then whooshed away into the night.

In Chip's hand the magic key began glowing.

Before they left, they heard a shout from the farmhouse. "Hank! What's going on out there?"

Hank winked at the children. "Nothing, Pa. Go back to sleep!"